Jade E
COLORING BOOKS FOR EVERYONE

Thank you for purchasing our coloring book!

We hope you have a fun and relaxing experience when coloring.

Everyone who worked on this book appreciates your support.

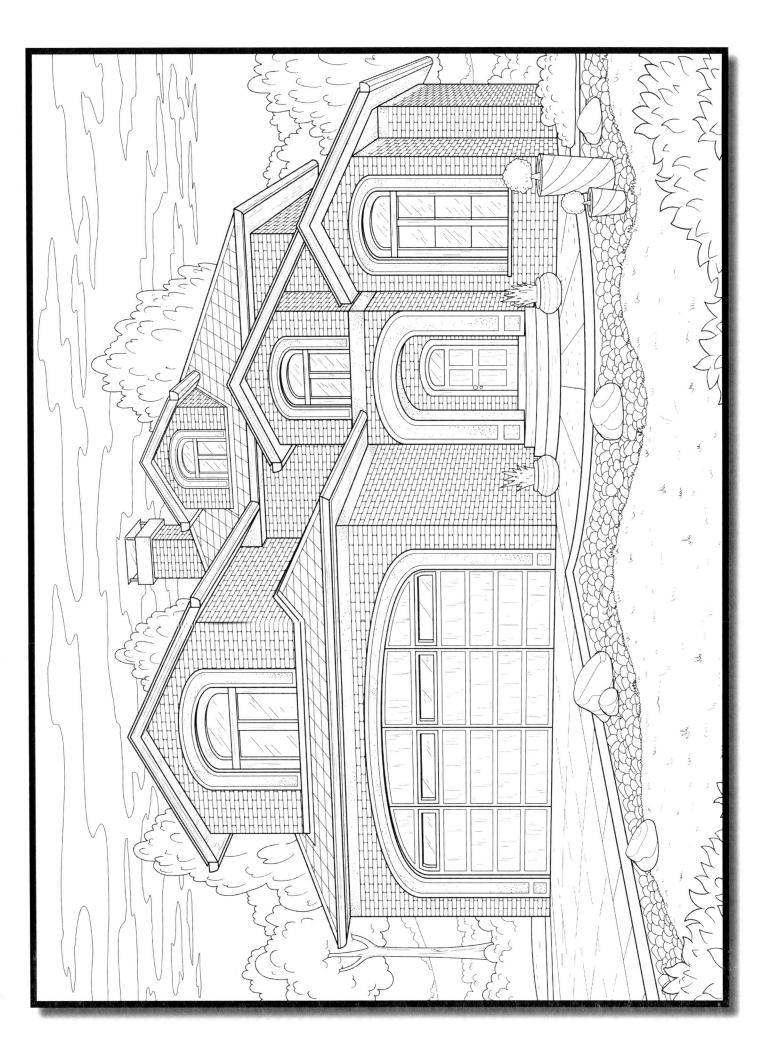

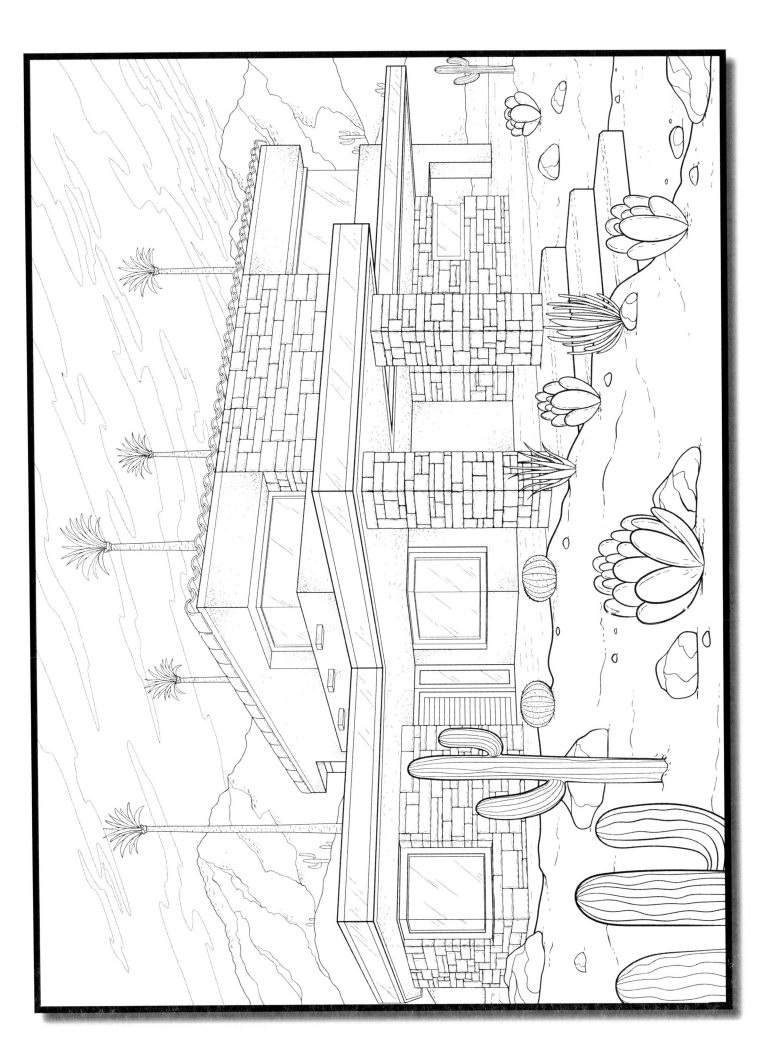

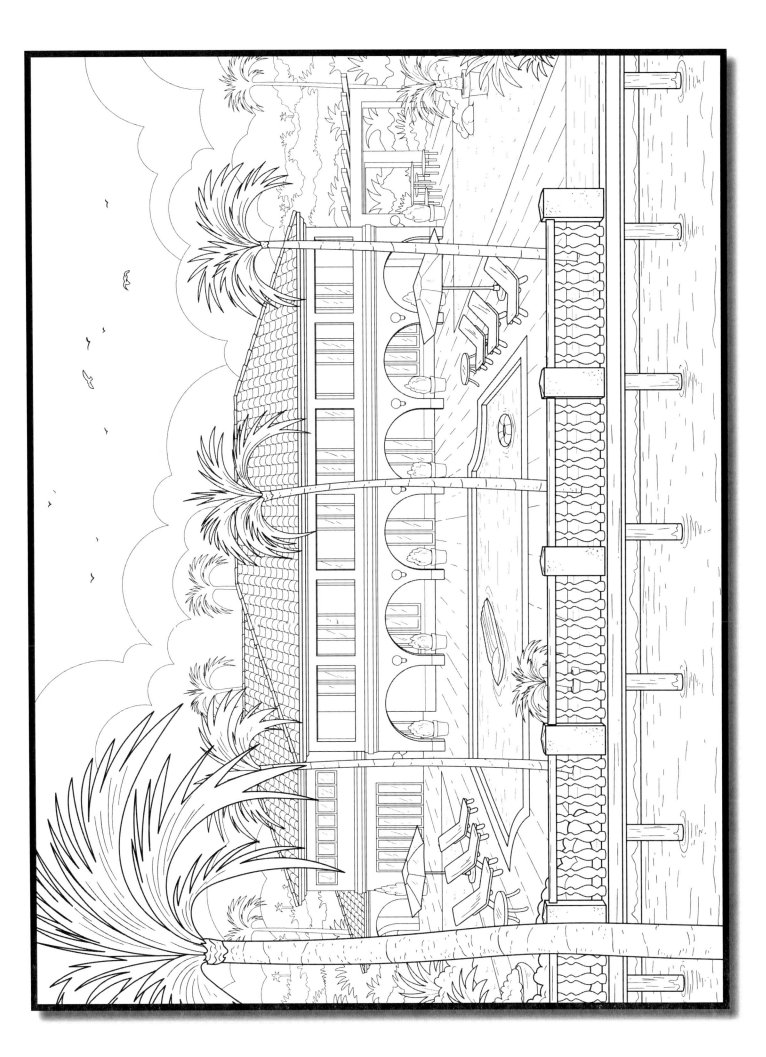

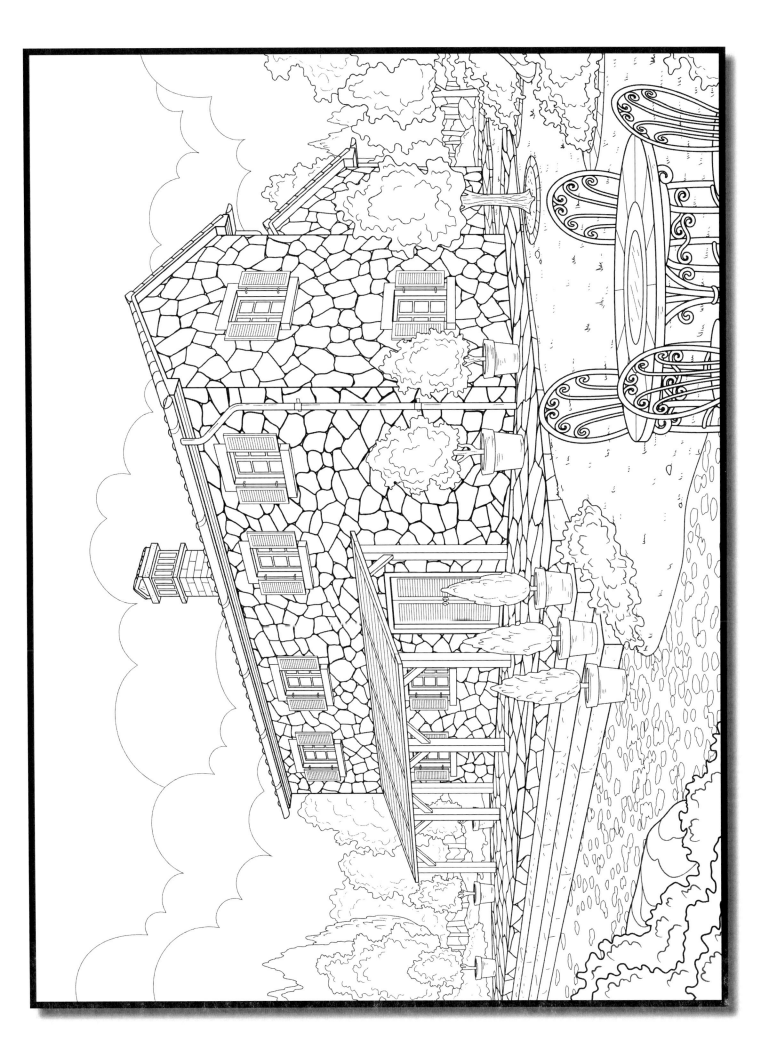

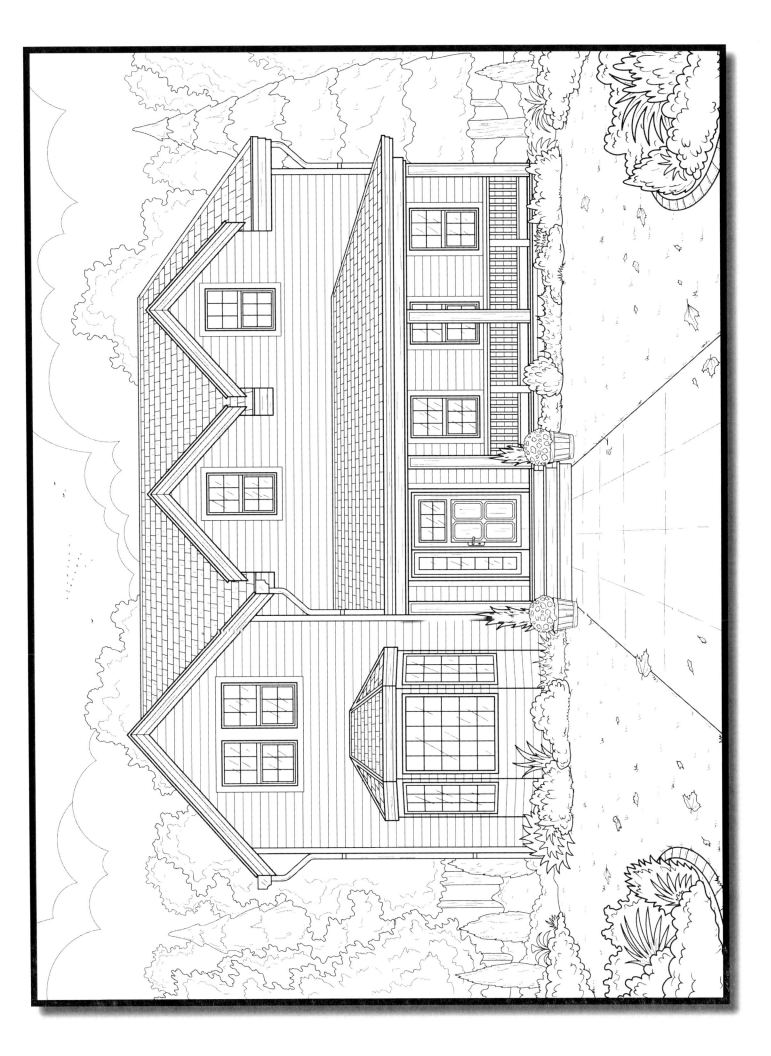

HOME EXTERIORS COLORING BOOK BY JADE SUMMER

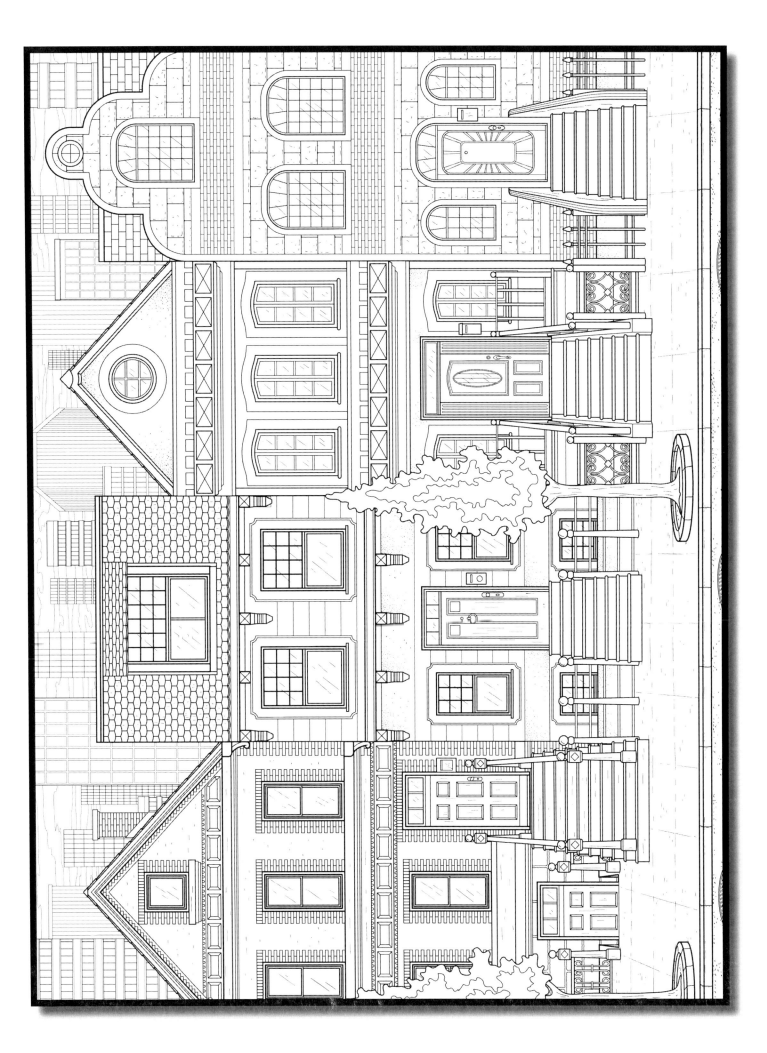

We have included a second copy of each image.

You can color your favorite images a second time, have an extra copy in case you make a mistake, or share one of our pages with a friend.

We hope this makes your coloring experience even better.

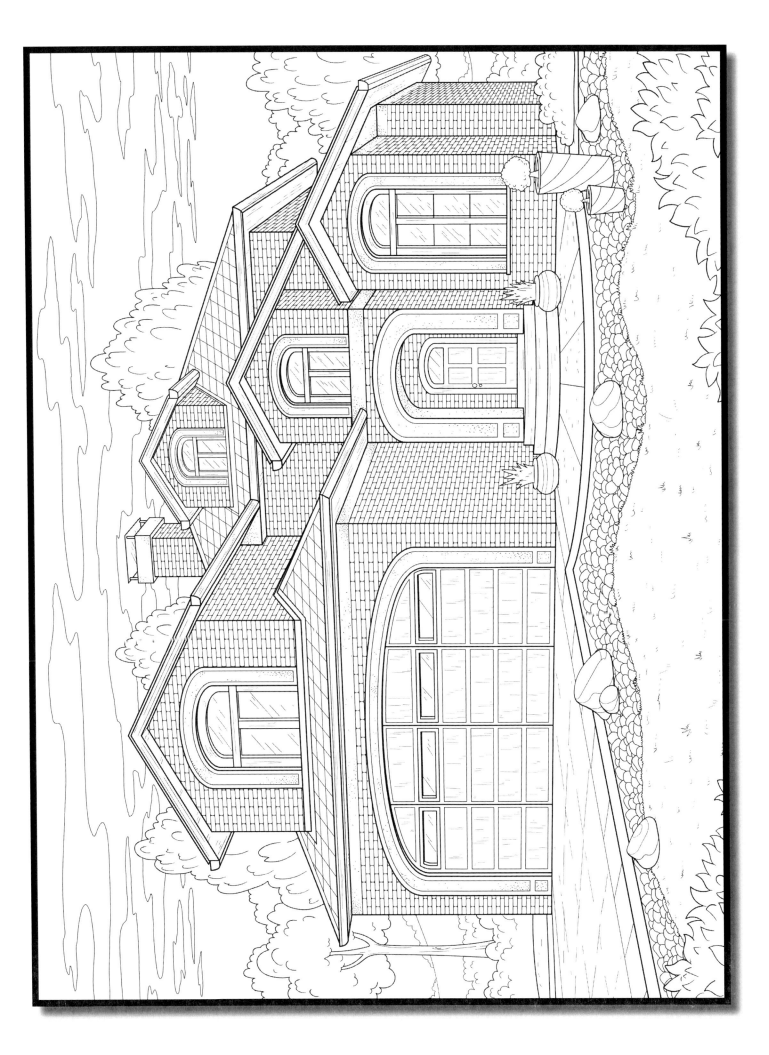

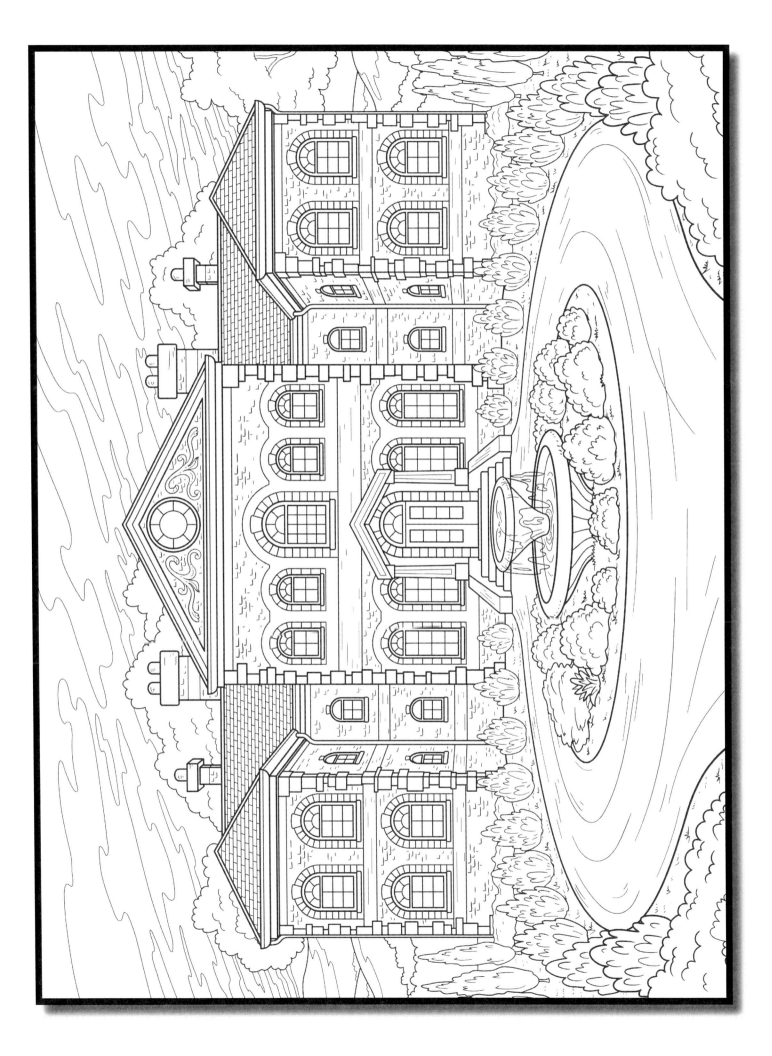

HOME EXTERIORS COLORING BOOK BY JADE SUMMER

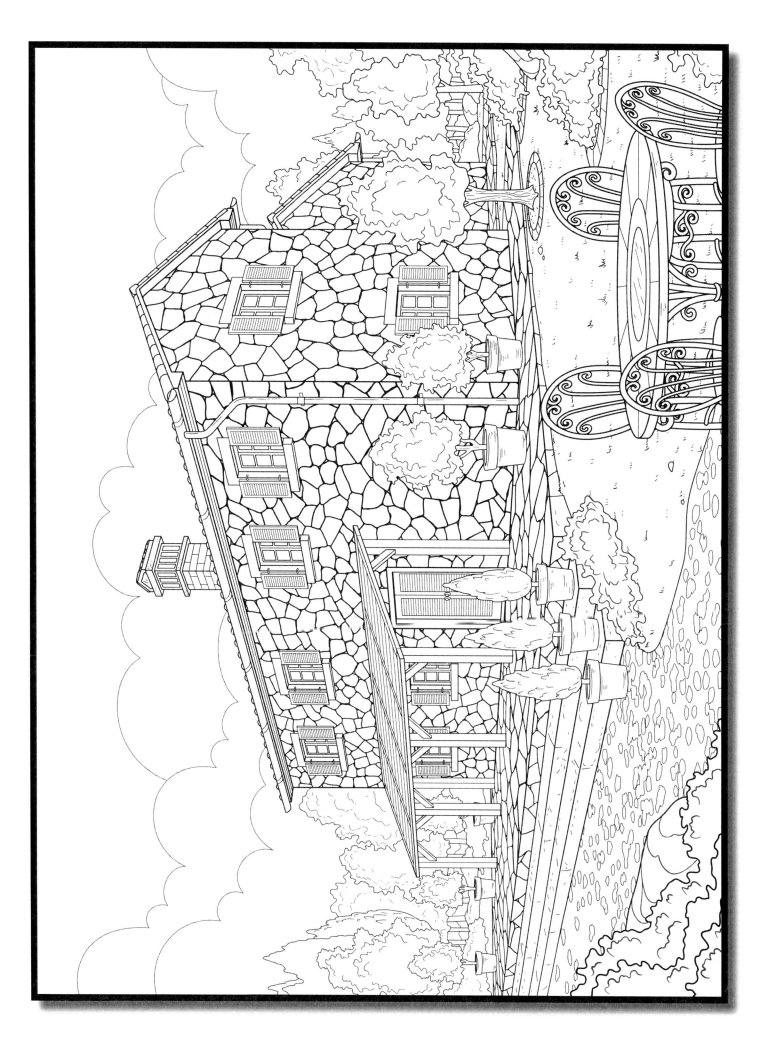

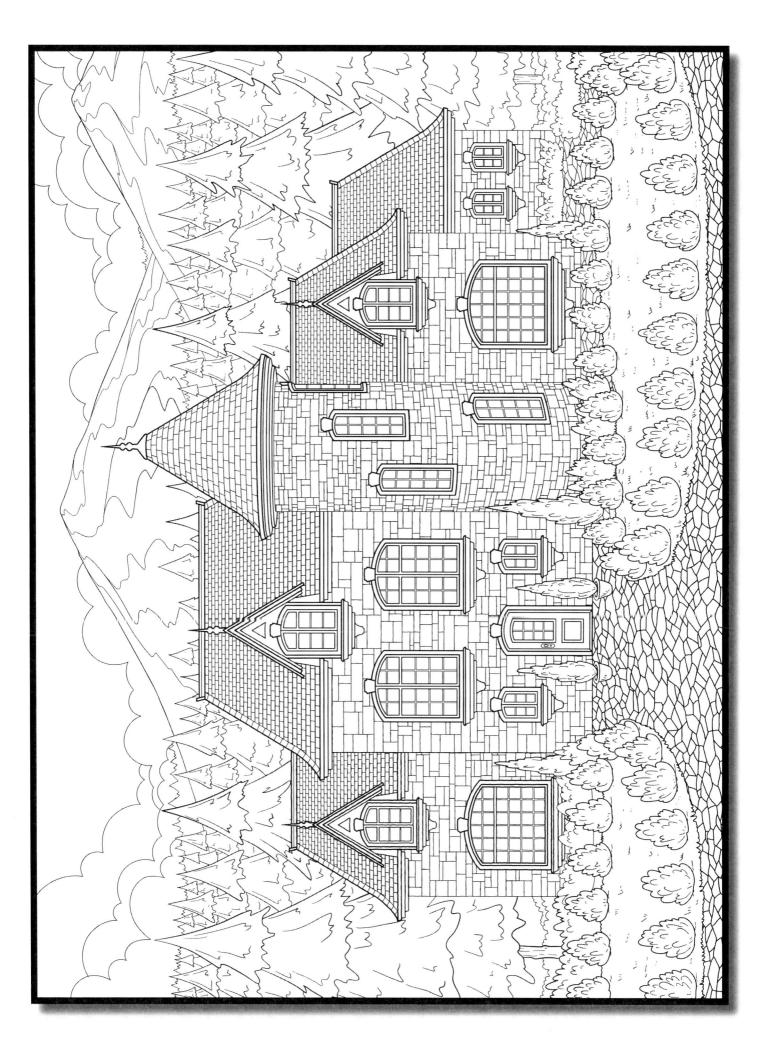

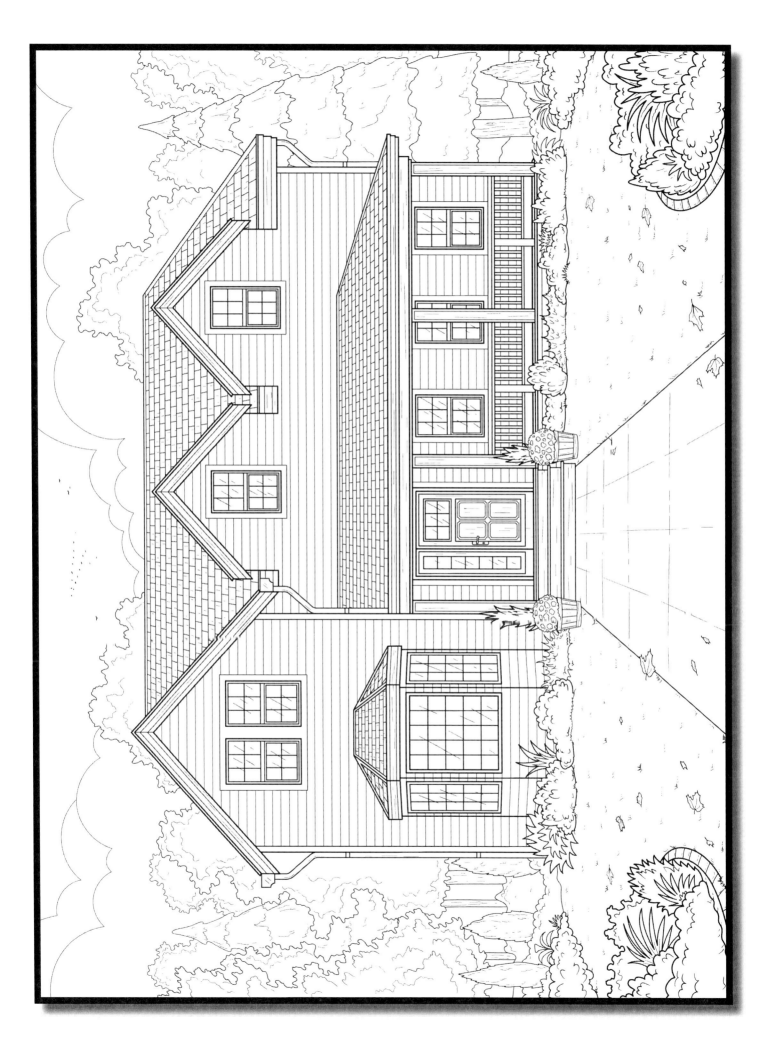

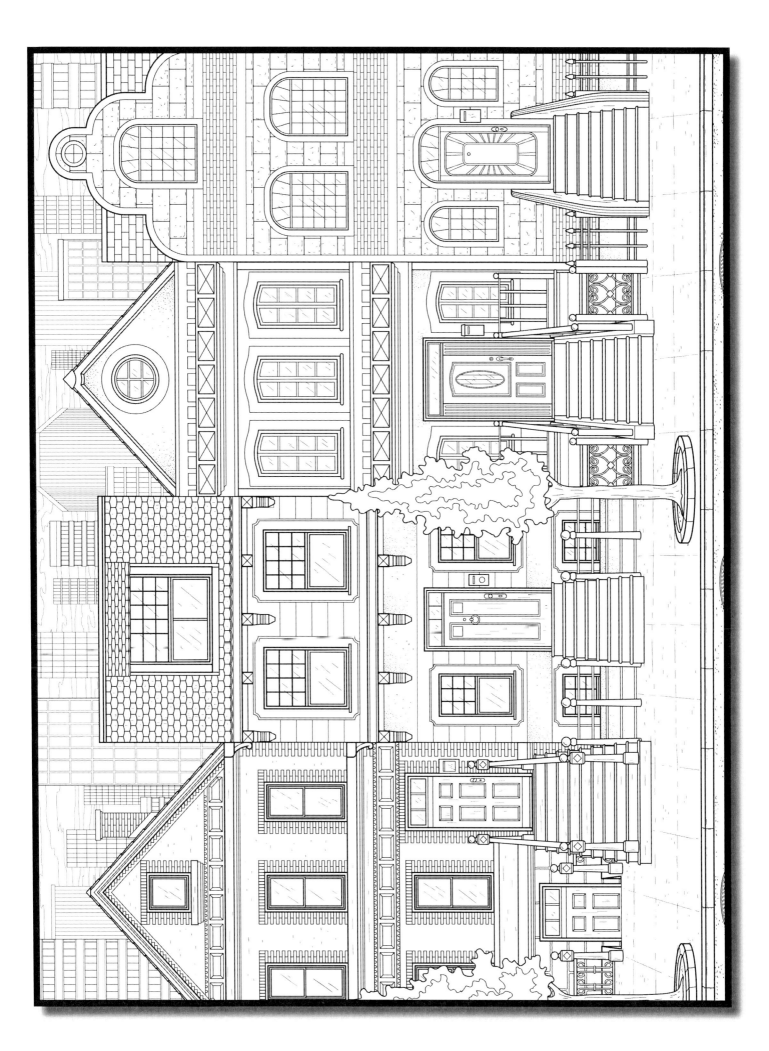

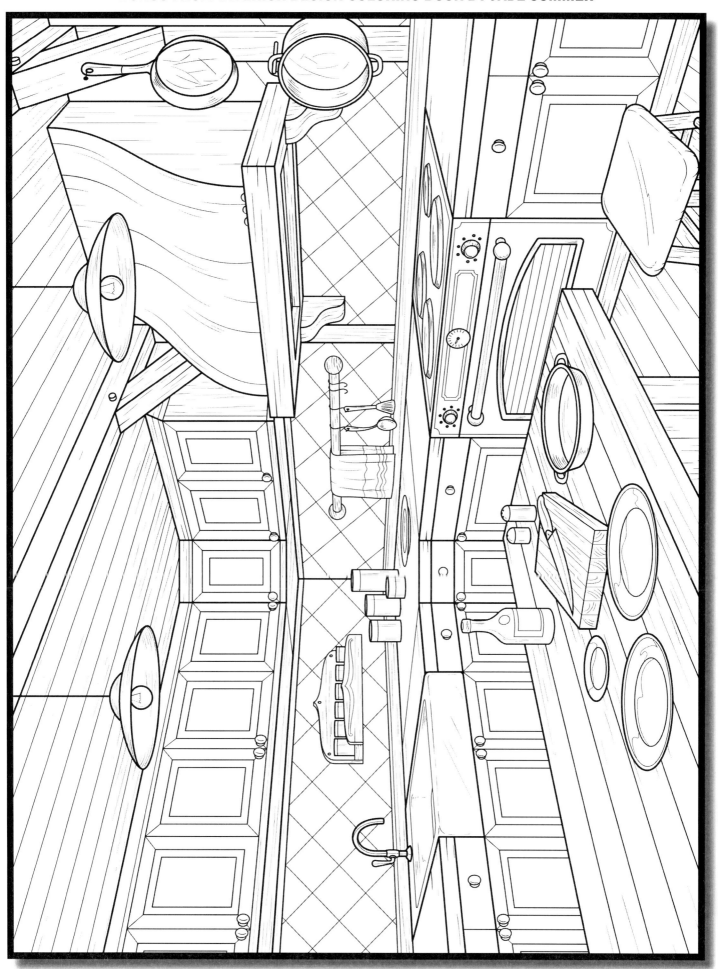

NOTES

This page is for testing and documenting your color choices.

Manufactured by Amazon.ca
Acheson, AB

10404000R00061